Point It Out!
TIPS FOR GREEN LIVING

The Eco-Shopper's Guide to

Buying Green

by J. Angelique Johnson

illustrated by Kyle Poling

PICTURE WINDOW BOOKS
a capstone imprint

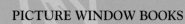

Going green means finding ways to keep our surroundings clean and healthy. These places include our homes, schools, communities, and world. One of the ways we can protect our surroundings is to shop smart. It takes energy to make everything we buy. When we shop smart, we make healthful choices for our bodies, the bodies of others, and Earth. That's what going green is all about!

Check out ways you can become an eco-shopper by looking closely at each area of the store throughout the pages of this book.

Groceries

Health & Beauty

Home & Kitchen

Office Suppl

Big Box

Jewelry

Electronics

Toys

Greeting Cards

Party Supplies

Bike Repair

Garden Center

3

Did You Know...

AMERICANS THROW AWAY ABOUT 18 BILLION DIAPERS EACH YEAR. THE DIAPERS CREATE HEAPS OF PLASTIC IN LANDFILLS.

Way to Go!

That shampoo bottle is recyclable in your area. By recycling plastic, you'll help save resources.

Cotton Balls

Oh, No!

Those cotton balls have been bleached. Look for unbleached, organic cotton products instead.

Oh, No!
Don't buy that toilet cleaner. Chemicals from cleaning products can pollute our waterways. Instead, use baking soda to clean toilets.

Oh, No!
That toilet paper isn't made from recycled paper. To help save trees, buy toilet paper that is made from mostly recycled paper.

Biodegradable

Garbage Bags

Toilet Paper

Way to Go!
You picked up biodegradable garbage bags. They break down naturally in landfills.

Oh, No!
Don't buy that bleach-based cleaning product. Bleach is harmful to the environment. You can use vinegar and water to clean surfaces in your home.

Bleach

Oh, No!
Don't buy new clothing yet. Head to a thrift store first. There you might find clothing, toys, dinnerware, and even furniture. It's a great way to reuse!
Oh, No!
Shopping for new jewelry? Think about buying used jewelry instead. Mining precious metals and gems uses a lot of resources.
PANTS / JEANS
SHIRTS
REUSABLE TOTES
$1.00
Way to Go!
You're reducing waste by placing goods in reusable cotton totes. Paper and plastic bags take up space in landfills.

Way to Go!

You're buying a laptop computer. Laptops use less energy than desktop computers. To save even more resources, buy a used laptop.

Way to Go!

Recycle batteries and cell phones at a service desk in stores that provide this service.

Oh, No!

Don't buy individual CDs. Reduce waste by downloading music to an MP3 player.

15

Way to Go!

You're looking at a refrigerator with a built-in water filtration system. With filtered water in your home, you might be less likely to buy bottled water. You'll help reduce the amount of plastic in landfills.

Way to Go!

See that Energy Star label? You're choosing an appliance that will use less energy than one without the label.

ENERGY STAR

Way to Go!

That's recycled printer paper. You help save trees and cut down on pollution when you buy recycled paper.

ECO Office Supplies

Way to Go!

You're recycling ink cartridges at the service desk. By doing so, you'll help keep plastic out of landfills.

Way to Go!

Go for recycled and eco-friendly office supplies. Look for pens, mouse pads, paper clips, and scissors made with recycled plastics.

18

Oh, No!
Don't waste paper. Let that special someone know how much you care by sending them an e-card.

Greeting Cards

Oh, No!
Don't buy that new gift bag. Reduce waste by wrapping gifts with dish towels, old posters, or newspaper. If you receive a gift wrapped in paper, save the paper and reuse it.

By shopping smart, you'll protect Earth's natural resources. Some resources, such as wind power, are renewable. That means they will never run out, no matter how much of them we use. Other resources, such as oil, can run out. We must be careful how much of these resources we use.

Protect Earth's natural resources by becoming an eco-shopper. The next time you're at the store, think about ways you can shop green.

Glossary

biodegradable—a substance or object that breaks down naturally in the environment

bulk—in large amount

compact fluorescent lightbulb (CFL)—a low-energy lightbulb

compost—a mixture of dead leaves, grass clippings, and even kitchen scraps that are mixed together to make fertilizer

environment—everything surrounding people, animals, and plants

fertilizer—a substance added to soil to make plants grow better

landfill—land set aside where garbage is dumped and buried

livestock—animals raised on a farm for food and profit, such as cows, pigs, horses, and sheep

mine—to dig up minerals that are underground

organic—using only natural products and no chemicals

pollution—harmful materials that damage the air, water, and soil

precious metal—a kind of metal that has value, like gold

resources—things that can be used to keep other things or people functioning; wind, sunlight, soil, and water are all examples of resources

VOCs—chemicals that change quickly from liquid to vapor; they pollute the air and are harmful to humans; *VOCs* stands for volatile organic compounds

water filtration system—a system that removes harmful materials from water

waterway—a place where water travels, such as rivers, streams or canals

To Learn More

More Books to Read

Martin Jr., Bill, and Michael Sampson. *I Love Our Earth*. Watertown, Mass.: Charlesbridge, 2006.

Nagle, Jeanne. *Smart Shopping: Shopping Green*. Your Carbon Footprint. New York: Rosen Central, 2009.

Orme, Helen. *Living Green*. Earth in Danger. New York: Bearport Pub., 2009.

Internet Sites

FactHound offers a safe, fun way to find Internet sites related to this book. All of the sites on FactHound have been researched by our staff.

Here's all you do:
Visit *www.facthound.com*
Type in this code: 9781404860292

Index

Look for all of the books in the Point It Out! Tips for Green Living series:

The Eco-Family's Guide to Living Green
The Eco-Neighbor's Guide to a Green Community
The Eco-Shopper's Guide to Buying Green
The Eco-Student's Guide to Being Green at School

Special thanks to our advisers for their expertise:

Rebecca Meyer, Extension Educator
4-H Youth Development
University of Minnesota Extension, Cloquet

Terry Flaherty, PhD, Professor of English
Minnesota State University, Mankato

Editor: Shelly Lyons
Designer: Alison Thiele
Art Director: Nathan Gassman
Production Specialist: Jane Klenk

The illustrations in this book were created digitally.
Photo Credit: Shutterstock/Doodle, 22

Picture Window Books
151 Good Counsel Drive
P.O. Box 669
Mankato, MN 56002-0669
877-845-8392
www.capstonepub.com

Printed in the United States of America, North Mankato,
Minnesota. 032010 005740CGF10

 All books published by Picture Window Books
are manufactured with paper containing at least
10 percent post-consumer waste.

Library of Congress Cataloging-in-Publication Data

Johnson, J. Angelique.
The eco-shopper's guide to buying green / by J. Angelique
Johnson, illustrated by Kyle Poling.
p. cm. — (Point it out! tips for green living)
Includes bibliographical references and index.
ISBN 978-1-4048-6029-2 (library binding)
1. Environmentalism—Juvenile literature. 2. Sustainable
living—Juvenile literature. 3. Shopping—Environmental
aspects—Juvenile literature. I. Poling, Kyle ill. II. Title.
GE195.5.J34 2011
640—dc22   2010015692